Everything I Know I Learned in My Garden

Emilie Barnes

WITH ANNE CHRISTIAN BUCHANAN

PAINTINGS BY **Susan Rios**

HARVEST HOUSE™ PUBLISHERS

EUGENE, OREGON

BS MS CCU LD GB

Everything I Know I Learned in My Garden

Text Copyright © 2003 by Harvest House Publishers
Eugene, OR 97402

ISBN 0-7369-1001-8

Original Artwork © Susan Rios. Licensed by Art Impressions, Canoga Park, CA.
For more information regarding artwork featured in this book, please contact Susan Rios, Inc.,
(818) 995-7467 or www.susanriosinc.com.

Design and production by Garborg Design Works, Minneapolis, Minnesota

Portions of this book are excerpted from *Time Began in a Garden* (Harvest House Publishers, 1995).

Unless otherwise indicated, all Scripture quotations are taken from the Holy Bible: New International
Version®. NIV®. Copyright © 1973, 1978, 1984 by the International Bible Society. Used by permis-
sion of Zondervan Publishing House. The "NIV" and "New International Version" trademarks are
registered in the United States Patent and Trademark Office by International Bible Society.

Printed in Hong Kong

04 05 06 07 08 09 10 11 12 / NG / 10 9 8 7 6 5 4 3

Everything I Know I Learned in My Garden...

Begin early. But it's never too late to start.

If it doesn't work, try something else.

Life is fragile. Protect it.

Life is enduring. Trust it.

Life is daily. Water it. Weed it.

Life is indescribably beautiful. Enjoy it and say thank you.

Growth takes time. And while you're waiting, pull a weed.

There's something for everybody—different blooms for different rooms.

Pruning hurts. Pruning helps you grow.

Sometimes the tiniest flowers smell the sweetest.

To everything there is a season. But know what season you're in.

Dream big. But try not to let ambition turn your joy into drudgery.

Grow what you love. The love will keep it growing.

You reap what you sow. But there will be surprises.

Begin early.
But it's never too late to start.

Even if she forgets the whole thing in her teens, later still, when she is grown up and has a first garden of her own, some misty memory of the pleasure of growing things will give her a headstart over the gardener without any background, just as children who have spoken a second language, and forgotten it, can pick it up again in later years.

—ANNE SCOTT-JAMES

Wake up!" the garden calls to me—a command so gentle it almost feels like coaxing, like Mama shaking me tenderly after a too-long afternoon nap.

Wake up and smell the roses. And while you are sniffing, take in the fragrance of sweet peas, and orange blossoms—their delicate or heady fragrances mingling with the rich smell of earth and the tantalizing herbal aromas of basil and thyme.

Garden time is time that involves itself in the moment, that passes each moment fully alive, that focuses on the soaring stateliness of trees and the minute scale of the tiniest blossom and insect. Garden time requires daily attention but does not require that everything be done in a day.

How could such sweet and wholesome hours be reckoned but in herbs and flowers?
—ANDREW MARVELL

Come away from your rat race, your conveyor belt, your traffic jam, to be renewed and refreshed in the company of growing things. It won't take long, but it will feel like a day in the country. You're on garden time now. It's time the way God created it: as a servant and not a master.

I hope you will make time to be in the garden. I hope you will take the time to be still and experience the paradise you have helped create.

And if you really don't have the time or the space or the inclination to start and maintain a garden, I hope you will find a way to have a flower in your life, even if only by reading about it or by purchasing a bouquet from a street vendor.

SusanRios

If it doesn't work, try something else.

We also glory in tribulations, knowing that tribulation produces perseverance;
and perseverance, character; and character, hope. Now hope does not disappoint,
because the love of God has been poured out in our hearts...

—THE BOOK OF ROMANS

*I*f a plant doesn't work in one place, it must be moved, and we've sometimes had to discard a bush or a tree that just didn't look or grow right. And, of course, we must watch for weeds, sometimes sacrificing the life of one plant for another.

I have to do that with the growing issues of my life as well. When I try to break a bad habit or acquire a new good one, or I try to mend a broken relationship or build a new friendship, I can't expect instant results. I must simply do what I know to do, then patiently wait for the results. My experience in the garden tells me that the results will probably be worthwhile—I'll either achieve my objective, or I'll learn something I needed to learn.

Love of gardening is a seed that once sown never dies, but always grows and grows to an enduring and ever-increasing source of happiness...

Each new step becomes a little surer, and each new grasp a little firmer, till, little by little, comes the power of intelligent combination, the nearest thing we know to the mighty force of creation.

—GERTRUDE JEKYLL

Garden lessons are one of gardening's great joys—equal almost to the joy of seeing one's dreams gradually unfurl into green reality.

We gardeners are always in the process of picturing the next phase of our perennial borders or the newest choice for our cutting gardens or next year's plans for our vegetable plots. We are continually assessing what has gone right and what has gone wrong and what might work better and what would be simply wonderful.

"Perhaps another row of larkspur there—and I need a taller varietal."

"I think we could put in an arbor with climbing roses and morning glories— and I want some zinnias for the house."

"That color of cosmos is definitely too much over by the porch, but wouldn't it be great out next to the fence?"

And by the time the bulb catalogs arrive, we are hungry to begin dreaming of even more possibilities.

Lessons discovered in the fulfillment of our garden dreams are ever-renewing, a source of ongoing energy and passion. They are the impetus to our plans, the motivation that keeps us fighting the bugs and the weeds and the calluses.

Life is fragile. Protect it.

Most garden dreams thrive on hope—for what is a dream but imaginative hoping? And gardeners, as a group, are the most hopeful people I know.

It takes a measure of hope to make even the simplest beginning—to buy a little pot, a bag of soil. It takes a hopeful spirit to see anemones and chrysanthemums in a strip of undecorated sod or bare dirt, to envision daffodils when the eye sees only snow—even

Hope is the thing with feathers
That perches in the soul,
And sings the tune without the words,
And never stops at all...
—EMILY DICKINSON

to expect that a scrawny little bunch of leaves in a new pot will choose to grow and flower.

It takes hope, in other words, to start a garden.

But the garden itself is what really teaches you how to hope.

The hope in a gardener's heart is strengthened every year by the experience of watching green settle in a filmy veil over bare branches, watching a bare, raked plot of ground suddenly explode with busy, purposeful growth.

Not that there aren't disappointments…and the occasional heartbreak.

That expensive peony you've nurtured so carefully may never hold up its heavy head. Aphids and snails may defy your most diligent efforts. The neighbor's dog may dig up two feet of your prized perennial border. A whole year's peaches may turn out green and hard and sour.

But there's always next year.

You have another chance.

Now faith is being sure of what we hope for and certain of what we do not see.
—THE BOOK OF HEBREWS

❧

To me the garden is also a refuge, a place to go for rest and spiritual renewal. In the freeway of my life, I love to find an exit ramp that leads to a green retreat. There I can sit still or stroll slowly or dig in the soil and let the serenity of shrub and vine begin to grow inside me.

Be joyful in hope, patient in affliction, faithful in prayer.
—THE BOOK OF ROMANS

Life is enduring. Trust it.

See! The winter is past;
the rains are over and gone.
Flowers appear on the earth;
the season of singing has come,
the cooing of doves
is heard in our land...

—THE SONG OF SOLOMON

The most hopeful lesson I've learned in more than thirty years of gardening is that plants as a whole are far hardier and more forgiving than most people ever imagine. There are almost no fatal mistakes and very few serious ones. You always have a chance to start over.

Hope is nurtured every time a pruned-back bush sends forth invigorated shoots, every time a languishing bush flourishes in a new location, every

15

time a self-seeded volunteer crops up in a new location as a lovely surprise. Hope is nurtured just by being in the company of trees and plants and flowers, by witnessing the relentless strength and energy of growing things.

My friend Anne teaches an art class to a group of second graders. The first rule they must learn in the class is that no one is allowed to say, "I messed up." That doesn't mean that mistakes aren't allowed! But she wants them to learn that mistakes aren't fatal. So instead of saying, "I messed up," they learn to say, "I want to try again." Instead of dwelling on their failures, they are encouraged to say, "I'd like a new piece of paper."

That's exactly the way the garden works. You always have a fresh piece of paper. You can always try again.

Working in the garden gives me something beyond enjoyment of the senses....It gives me a profound feeling of inner peace. There is no rush toward accomplishment, no blowing of trumpets. Here is the great mystery of life and growth. Everything is changing, growing, aiming at something, but silently, unboastfully, taking its time.

—RUTH STOUT

Life is daily. Water it. Weed it.

"Just living is not enough," said the butterfly.
"One must have sunshine, freedom, and a little flower."
—HANS CHRISTIAN ANDERSEN

There are gardeners who love nothing better than wrestling with the elements: digging bare fingers deep in the soil, struggling with shovels, digging and redigging and planting and replanting, making and remaking their gardens as they strive toward the dream in their mind. They are the artists and the engineers of the garden; they thrive on the challenge of turning bare ground into something lovely and fruitful.

Other gardeners are the nurturers, who love to attend to growing things the way they attend to children. These men and women find a parent's joy in tucking the tiny seeds into beds and watching the tender shoots grow taller.

I hadn't been involved with plants for more than a season before I began to realize what was happening.

I had thought I was growing my garden, when actually my garden was growing me. Teaching me. Making me wiser.

> You care for the land and water it;
> you enrich it abundantly.
> The streams of God are filled with water
> to provide the people with grain,
> for so you have ordained it.
> You drench its furrows
> and level its ridges;
> you soften it with showers
> and bless its crops.
> You crown the year with your bounty,
> and your carts overflow with abundance.
>
> —THE BOOK OF PSALMS

I used to garden almost entirely for the results. I liked having flowers on my windowsill, so I knew I had to dig in the soil and plant the seeds and pull the weeds and drag around the watering hose. I loved picking fresh herbs and vegetables for my table, so I knew I had to fertilize and mulch and prune and pick. (Sometimes, in certain seasons, I have to pick and pick and pick!)

But the longer I'm involved with the garden, the more I'm learning to appreciate the process of gardening. And I'm coming to appreciate more and more the lessons my garden can teach me if I only pay attention.

Of course, I'm not the first person to discover

that the garden is really an institute of higher learning, the plants and flowers beautiful visual aids.

I think of the ancient Egyptians learning the lessons of watering and fertilizing around the Nile, of the wandering Hebrews learning the lay of the Promised Land, of Plato and Socrates and their students learning philosophy in the groves around Athens.

I think of Jesus advising the crowds to "consider the lilies of the field..." and learn from them.

I think of Aristotle's student Theophrastus, the father of botany, writing down the observations that influenced gardeners and scientists through the centuries...And I think of Bob and me, starting with pots of geraniums in our tiny apartment, planting trees and flower beds in our "starter" home, growing ferns and impatiens in our townhouse, putting in raised beds around the remodeled barn where we lived for many years.

So much to learn. So much growing to do. Every day.

> *One day, the gardener realizes that what she is doing out there is actually teaching herself to garden by performing a series of experiments. This is a pivotal moment.*
>
> —MARGARET ROACH

> *Is there any sense to the notion that a person has to know a subject from A to Z in order to begin teaching it effectively? If you are sure of your ground as far as you have gone, if you know the alphabet to M, let us say, you can teach that much of it can't you?...Following up that theory, in my third year of gardening I began to teach it. Next to working in my own garden I like starting ones for somebody else.*
>
> —RUTH STOUT

Life is indescribably beautiful.
Enjoy it and say thank you.

Every day my garden lavishes on me gifts of beauty and serenity and wonderful fragrance and succulent flavor.

My response is to say thank you, every single day. I want to keep remembering that all this is a gift. Even after I have worked to help bring it about, it's still a gift.

And then I have another response. I want to share.

The main reason I love to share my garden is that sharing multiplies my joy.

Bob and I bought our property in the

For flowers that bloom about our feet,
Father, we thank Thee;
For tender grass so fresh and sweet,
Father, we thank Thee.
For the song of bird and hum of bee,
For all things fair we hear or see,
Father in heaven, we thank Thee.

—RALPH WALDO EMERSON

first place with sharing in mind. We have plenty of room for conferences, open houses, and for overnight guests. We love to barbecue out in the garden, or just to have people over for tea and talk. And every time I look at my garden through the eyes of a visitor, I receive its gifts anew.

I'm far from the first person to discover this open secret about sharing. So many of the gardeners I know are openhearted sharers. They love to lavish the people around them with cuttings and bouquets and tomatoes and stories about their gardens.

The garden is a place to feel the beauty of solitude.
—BOB BARNES

Then God said, "I give you every seed-bearing plant on the face of the whole earth and every tree that has fruit with seed in it. They will be yours for food. And to all the beasts of the earth and all the birds of the air and all the creatures that move on the ground—everything that has the breath of life in it—I give every green plant for food." And it was so.
—THE BOOK OF GENESIS

The gardener's experience involves the deep satisfaction of working side by side with the Creator to develop a place of beauty, a safe and life-enhancing environment. The satisfaction of being a gardener is in part the satisfaction of working hard and seeing results. It is also the artist's satisfaction of envisioning something beautiful and rendering that beauty tangible. It is the satisfaction of making the world a better place, of participating in an activity that has been bettering the world for countless centuries.

The world will never starve for want of wonders.
—G.K. CHESTERTON

The Fragrant Garden

All the following flowers, herbs, and shrubs contribute to the lovely fragrance of a garden. Double flowers often put off a stronger scent. But be careful: not every variety of every flower listed will be fragrant. For example, some daffodils have almost no scent. Also, check with your local nursery to make sure your selections will grow well in your region.

alyssum
artemisia
butterfly bush
candytuft
chamomile
crocus
daffodil
daylily
flowering tobacco
four o'clock
freesia
gardenia
geranium
scented heliotrope
honeysuckle
hyacinth
iris
jasmine

lavender
lemon balm
lemon thyme
lemon verbena
lilac mignonette
mint
moonflower
narcissus
petunia
pinks
primrose
rose
sage
snowdrop

sweet pea
sweet woodruff
violet

Growth takes time. Be patient.
And while you're waiting, pull a weed.

Every gardener knows that under the cloak of winter lies a miracle...
a seed waiting to sprout, a bulb opening to the light, a bud straining to unfurl.
And the anticipation nurtures our dreams.

—BARBARA WINKLER

*T*here is so much my garden teaches. I've learned the value of good preparation and solid planning, of thinking ahead of the season and anticipating what is likely to happen. I use what I've learned as I fertilize the lawn ahead of coming rains, and as we contribute to our retirement programs.

But I've also learned to wait, which is a companion virtue. Even though I admit to being an impatient gardener, my garden has taught me many lessons in patience.

For me, the hardest part of gardening is the preparation. I get impatient with the process of digging, fertilizing, preparing the beds. I tend to want instant flowers. But that's not the way it works, in the garden or in life.

Even if you go to the garden center and buy three dozen pansy plants, you have to wait to get them home and planted, and before you do that you have to get their bed ready for them. And I really do want something besides pansies and mums in my garden. So I have to have patience. I have to do my job and then wait on the season, wait for the natural progression of growth.

But the fruit of the Spirit is love, joy, peace, patience, kindness, goodness, faithfulness, gentleness and self-control.
—THE BOOK OF GALATIANS

There's something for everybody—different blooms for different rooms.

Gently steed our spirits,
carrying with them dreams of flowers.

—WILLIAM WORDSWORTH

*I*n your dreams, how does your garden grow?

Is it a window box full of petunias and pinks like the ones you saw in Germany?

Is it a wandering path through blooming bushes, a series of surprises like you remember from your great-aunt's house?

Does your dream feature wisteria dripping from a trellis or roses climbing a garden gate or water lilies sunning themselves in a pond?

Or do you dream about pots of greenery in the corners of your rooms and graceful bouquets gracing your tabletops?

All this is important to consider because your dreams are where your garden begins.

More than anything, I must have flowers always, always.

—CLAUDE MONET

Some people who garden simply want a flower on the table, an herb in the stew, a tomato in the salad.

Some enjoy being garden scientists: testing the soil, experimenting with seeds and grafts, carefully recording the results.

There are homemakers, driven by their nesting instincts to surround their living space with beauty, and artists striving to paint an ever-changing picture with living, three-dimensional forms.

Some people garden for the challenge of raising the perfect rose, of placing the perfect row of graceful daylilies in front of the perfect stand of vigilant hollyhocks.

To pick a flower is so much more satisfying than just observing it, or photographing it...So in later years I have grown in my garden as many flowers as possible for children to pick.

—ANNE SCOTT-JAMES

Some respond to the call of ever-renewing life, because they are invigorated and renewed by being involved with such an astounding miracle of growth.

And some people garden simply because they love being in a garden, and gardening is the best way they know to get there.

"Might I," quavered Mary, "might I have a bit of earth?"...

"Earth!" he repeated. "What do you mean?"

"To plant seeds in—to make things grow—to see them come
*   alive," Mary faltered....*

"You can have as much earth as you want," he said. "You remind
*   me of some one else who loved the earth and things that*
*   grow. When you see a bit of earth you want," with*
*   something like a smile, "take it, child, and make it come alive."*

— FRANCES HODGSON BURNETT
The Secret Garden

Pruning hurts.
Pruning helps you grow.

Vulnerable, naked against the starlight, my tree looks unable to withstand the winter yet to come. I have done all I can. Spring will tell if the cuts will heal, if the scars will be buried in blossoms.

—CINDY CROSBY
Waiting for Morning

Pruning is a learning issue for me in the garden. On our property we have maybe three hundred trees of different varieties: fruit trees and shade trees, sycamores and ashes and pepper trees, even a beautiful olive tree. Every few years, Bob will call the tree trimmer, and I don't like to be there when it happens. Trimming always seems so brutal, like butchering the trees. Our fruitless mulberry trees are nothing but woody nubs when the trimmer is finished.

But as painful as the trimming process is, I have learned it pays big results. The trunk becomes stronger, and the foliage comes in lush and green. It always amazes me when those big branches and huge leaves come out from those pruned-back mulberries.

There are many situations in our garden that call for that kind of "tough love." We have to thin out a bed of seedlings, ripping out some so that others have a chance for life.

Effort is only troublesome when you are bored.

—CHRISTOPHER LLOYD

There have been many times when I've needed the pruning and thinning and weeding lesson in my own life. Sometimes I have had to weed out harmful activities that hurt my health or sapped my time and energy. Often I have had to think out my schedule to make room for what I really want. And there have been a few times when I had to take out the pruning hook, making radical cut-backs in areas of my life that were unsightly or unnecessary or just leading in the wrong direction. Once or twice I have even had to prune back my life to the very basics, using this time of curtailment to store up my strength and remember who I am.

Now, I'll have to admit that I wasn't always the one imposing these disciplines on myself, at least not consciously. Sometimes life did it for me. But looking back, I can see it had to be done. I am trying to see the opportunities for pruning ahead of time and to make wiser decisions about what to pull and cut and hoe.

> *For, before the harvest, when the blossom is gone*
> *and the flower becomes a ripening grape,*
> *he will cut off the shoots with pruning knives,*
> *and cut down and take away the spreading branches.*
> *They will all be left to the mountain birds of prey*
> *and to the wild animals;*
> *the birds will feed on them all summer,*
> *the wild animals all winter.*
>
> —THE BOOK OF ISAIAH

Pruning is just one of the many lessons my garden has taught me—some hard, some pure delight, many just instructive. I've learned hope, and joy, and wonder. I've learned about the value and rewards of work. I've learned volumes about the ways things grow, about the way the world is structured, and now I'm learning ways to be more responsible for the world: conserving water, cutting back on pesticides, recycling wastes.

For the most part, I'm a happy pupil.

35

Sometimes the tiniest flowers smell the sweetest.

"The color of the buttercups helps me to know that they are buttercups, but I might make a mistake if they were like some other flowers in size and shape."

"That is probably the way the bees know them," Uncle Jack added.

"But there are some flowers that are so small and have such little color you can hardly see them," Marylee objected.

"That is true," Uncle Jack agreed, "but most of those flowers have a strong perfume instead of large size and bright colors. The perfume helps the bees to find and know them."

—CHARLES H. GABLE AND ELLEN SCHULZ QUILLIN
From Seed to Tree

My garden exudes fragrances that soothe, fragrances that delight, fragrances that linger: a drift of honeysuckle, a waft of orange blossoms, a heady whiff of roses.

My garden nurtures my sense of wonder as well. The longer I linger, the more there is to see, to smell, to hear and touch and taste and know and wonder about.

I've seen it a million times, and it still amazes me.

I even know a little bit about why and how the garden happens, yet the wonder of it doesn't fade.

I obtain a little seed, perhaps a tiny speck so minuscule I have to mix it with sand or cornmeal to work with it. Fluffing up the soil, I dig a little hole, deposit the seed, and cover it cozily. A little water, a little compost, a little waiting. And before long something green and alive is poking its slender head up out of the soil.

It seems almost trite to call it a miracle, but it is one.

And the miracles happen dependably in my garden, day after day.

> *More than half a century has passed, and yet each spring, when I wander into the primrose wood and see the pale yellow blooms, and smell their sweetest of scents. . .for a moment I am seven years old again and wandering in the fragrant wood.*
> —GERTRUDE JEKYLL

To everything there is a season.
But know what season you're in.

I come to the garden alone…" begins the old gospel song. And I do that often—in times of pain or difficulty, or when I just need to think. For me, the garden path has always led to serenity, peacefulness, beauty, and yes, sometimes tears. If I want to get away and my heart is hurting, I take a walk out among the orange trees or in the rose garden and let my tears flow. I inevitably return with a sense of comfort, a renewed perspective, and fresh energy to try again.

It was not in the Winter
Our loving lot was cast;
It was the time of roses—
We pluck'd them as we pass'd!
—THOMAS HOOD

But I come to the garden in company, too, to share the enjoyment of cool, fragrant breezes and sunny smiles. I love to sit with my Bob out on the patio in the mornings, sharing a cup of coffee or tea and a thought for the day. I love to walk my granddaughter Christine out to the English garden or to the rose arbor to gather a bouquet, teaching her what my auntie told me. I love to wander with a friend under the trees and talk about what is happening in our lives. And I'm always game for spreading a blanket on the lawn or in the tree house for an impromptu picnic.

Of course, I have also been re-created while on my knees digging or weeding. There is no law that says you can't experience your garden while you're working in it. In fact, garden work is a perfect setting for re-creation. The combination of fresh air, exercise, and the company of plants is a tonic for the spirit.

There is a time for everything,
and a season for every activity under heaven:
a time to be born and a time to die,
a time to plant and a time to uproot,
a time to kill and a time to heal,
a time to tear down and a time to build,
a time to weep and a time to laugh,
a time to mourn and a time to dance,
a time to scatter stones and a time to gather them,
a time to embrace and a time to refrain,
a time to search and a time to give up,
a time to keep and a time to throw away,
a time to tear and a time to mend,
a time to be silent and a time to speak,
a time to love and a time to hate,
a time for war and a time for peace.

—THE BOOK OF ECCLESIASTES

Dream big. But try not to let ambition turn your joy into drudgery.

I found in dreams a place of wind and flowers,
Full of sweet trees and the color of glad grass...
—ALGERNON CHARLES SWINBURNE

I find that my sense of humor flourishes in the garden. Bob and I laugh together more easily when we're walking in the garden or working together—and the laughter is free, joyful, without sarcasm or cynicism. I don't know why this is, but it must have something to do with perspective, with balance—and because a garden invariably infects me with a sense of playfulness.

Yes, I know there's work to get done. And we get it done, one way or the other. But surely we are missing half the point of gardening if we miss the pleasure and the play that is part of the work.

Standing in my garden, breathing in deep and sweet, I realize how often I seem to be holding my breath. What a relief to find a place where the trees and plants have helped to cleanse the air, where taking a deep breath feels safe and pleasurable. (And what an important reason to keep growing plants, as well as taking steps to nourish the air we breathe!)

But this is not just a matter of breathing cleaner air. It's about finding a place where it's safe to feel. We're buffeted by bad news, harangued with hurry, assaulted with anxiety, until we unconsciously pull down our awareness levels like blinds on a too-bright window. No wonder we forget to breathe deeply! No wonder our spirits get hardened to the point that we can discern only the harshest of realities.

> *If seeds in the black earth can turn into such beautiful roses, what might not the heart of man become in its long journey toward the stars?*
> —G.K. CHESTERTON

But the garden is a safe place to reverse that hardening process, to become conversant with realities that are no less valid for being softer and more beautiful. A garden is a place of tenderness, of freshness, of joy and delight. The triumphs and sorrows here are on the scale of centuries, grounded in the eternal rhythms of the earth.

Grow what you love.
The love will keep it growing.

Over the years, my garden has sprouted with geraniums, peonies, and roses. I have plucked delicious fresh lemons, avocados, and oranges. But I know, too, that my garden's harvest includes a child's wonder, a friend's laughter, and my husband's smile. Among its shaded corners, raised beds, and trellis-lined paths, my garden grows love.

Our children have grown with the garden; every niche has been nursery, governess, and playmate.... My garden has been a pirate ship, Barbie Doll vacation paradise, Sylvanian Family campground, jungle, maze, obstacle course, arena for birthday treasure hunts, and the Yukon for Calvin and Hobbes. It is well peopled.

—SANDY PUCKETT

It's no secret that children and gardens just naturally go together. And grow together. The garden is outside in the fresh air, and so much is going on there. In fact, the garden is a completely stocked science lab where even the tiniest child can begin learning the basics of botany, biology, even chemistry. They learn that tiny seeds can grow into big trees, that plants make food in their leaves and drink through their roots, that flowers, like children, need food and drink and sunlight and love.

Working together with children is a great way to grow relationships—there's something about the rhythm of digging and weeding that makes sharing more natural and coaxes out confidences. Work becomes much more meaningful (even fun) for kids when it brings tangible rewards such as fresh vegetables and flowers. Our grandchildren love to pick their own dinner, bringing in the fruits and vegetables for me to wash and cook. And they are far more motivated to eat the right kind of food when they had a hand in growing it.

You reap what you sow.
But there will be surprises.

Sow for yourselves righteousness,
reap the fruit of unfailing love...
—THE BOOK OF HOSEA

You can learn a lot about gardening in books. You can even watch videos and TV shows, but gardening is also the ultimate hands-on learning experience. Hands on, Bob and I have learned an astonishing amount about our home and the land that surrounds it.

We've learned other things as well. We're not the first gardeners to discover that garden lessons reach far beyond the confines of the garden walls. In the laboratory of our garden, I have learned many beautiful, sometimes painful, lessons about how the world is ordered, about how I can live my life better.

Bob says that people who do a good job of managing their lives probably do a good job of managing their gardens, too. But the reverse is also true, I've found. Learning to manage a garden teaches you a lot about managing your life.

Lord, give me the serenity to accept the things I can't change, the courage to change the things I can, and the wisdom to know the difference.
—SERENITY PRAYER

I've heard it said that the most difficult task in life is learning what we can control and what we can't control—then acting appropriately. Most of us need help walking the fine line between helplessness and overcontrol!

My garden helps me learn to walk that fine line more gracefully.

If I want to have a garden, I must take the responsibility to prepare the soil, to plant the seedlings or the bulbs, to mulch and weed and water and feed. I must watch out for disease and for harmful insects and for extremes of weather. If I neglect any of those responsibilities, my garden will pay the price.

And yet I can do all those things and still have a bad year in the garden. A hailstorm or a flood or an infestation of hornworms can wipe out an entire crop or a whole section of my perennial border. The neighbor's dog (or my own dog) can go digging in my freshly planted cutting garden. Or rabbits can eat my tulip bulbs. Or I can nurture a tree or a shrub or a bed with the tenderest care and still have it die for no apparent reason.

I can do everything right, in other words, but cannot guarantee success. The results are out of my hands.

That's why I have learned to think of our garden as a gift, despite the hard work that Bob and I put into it...we cannot force good results. Still, the results in our garden so often are good, and that is a wonderful gift.